This book is for

....

Thank you for being the
greatest of friends
Love from,

....

Friends make the world beautiful

True friends are never apart, maybe in distance, but never in heart

A good friend knows all of your stories, a best friend has lived them with you

It's the friends we meet along the way that help us appreciate the journey

Friends are our chosen family

Good friends are like stars, you can't always see them, but you always know they are there

Friendship is not about who you have known for the longest, its about who comes into your life and is here for you, and proves it

A true friend sees the pain in your eyes, when everyone else sees the smile on your face

Friends buy you lunch, best friends eat your lunch!

Our laughs are limitless,
our memories are
countless, our friendship
is endless

True friendship takes us by the hand, and reminds us we are not alone in this journey

A friend is someone who
understands your past,
believes in your future,
and accepts you today,
the way that you are

Good friends help you to find important things when you've lost them: your smile, your hope, your courage

Good friends don't let you do stupid things. Alone!

Sometimes having fun
with a friend is the best
therapy

We will be best friends forever, because you already know too much!

When I count my blessings, I count you twice

We didn't realise we were making memories, we just knew we were having fun

A good friend knows you are a good egg, even if they can see you're slightly cracked

I'll be here for you no matter what

Thank you for always
being there for me

Always remember:
I'm here,
I'll wait,
I love you

You make each day a special day, just by being you

A problem shared is a problem halved

Coffee and friends are the perfect blend

Choose people who
choose you

There is only one happiness in this life, to love and to be loved

We will be the old people causing trouble at the nursing homes

I'll always pick you up
when you fall, once I've
finished laughing

Thank you for being you

Here's to many more
years of fun and
friendship!

Printed in Great Britain
by Amazon